WHAT TIME IS KICK OFF?

WHAT TIME IS KICK OFF?

STARTING, BUILDING AND GROWING YOUR OWN BUSINESS.

Michael R Middleton

ISBN-13: 9781540804099
ISBN-10: 1540804097

CONTENTS

INTRODUCTION

The object of this book is to provide concise help and guidance for people going into business for the first time. Based on conversations I have had with more experienced business people some of the information has proved helpful to them. It was not my intention to create the definitive guide, frankly that would be a monumental task and there is a grave risk the reader would not finish the book.

For 27 years I have been in, started and run my own businesses, over that time I have experienced disappointment, failure and of course success. I have had plenty, of what former Manchester United manager Sir Alex Ferguson called "squeaky bum" moments.

Sometimes when working with others I wonder if it is those moments of fear that most energises and excites some serial entrepreneurs. It is the proof we are alive, the fear of failure, the knowledge that this risk or that might not work out motivates as much as it exhilarates. Reflecting on some of my own decisions I think this probably applies to me.

Of course in addition to moments of fear (sheer panic occasionally) and worry, there has been much enjoyment and satisfaction. This too is needed to keep us going.

During my time in business I have started three new ventures, bought and sold a business and through the course of my career I have had the opportunity and privilege to work with many successful business owners and entrepreneurs. I have also had the fortune to be able to help them and of course learn from them. As I set out in the opening paragraph this book is intended to be short and is a distillation of what I have found works and does not work and the many ups and downs I and others have experienced.

All too often in the search for something magic, a silver bullet if you like, it is easy to look for complex reasons for other people's success so you too can copy them. Thousands of words, actually probably millions of words have been written on the subject of starting businesses and success. There have been countless academic studies on the subject, which in my experience few successful people have actually read, or if they have started frequently wind up not completing the book as they are too deep, or too long and worse, sometimes both. This search for complex reasons for success encourages us to ignore the simple, the obvious and as a consequence it frequently holds us back.

I am not seeking to denigrate academia, far from it, without a world of great engineers, mathematicians, medics and scientists I would not be in a position to write this book. However we ignore the simple at our peril and cost. In the words of the well-known sports brand Nike sometimes the answer is to just "Do it."

In many respects there is nothing new under the sun, for example the in the book of Genesis the first words of the first line are " In the beginning.....", Whether you are religious or not all things have a beginning, the book goes on to describe the creation of the earth. In other words to begin with there was nothing until it was created.

All successful businesses start at the beginning, with an idea. Most five year olds know this and perhaps because it sounds so utterly obvious and therefore maybe childish it leads many to ignore the beginning.

There might be people reading this now who will class me an idiot for making this observation and so do not read the rest of the book. They will give it up instantly. Which is ironic as the most common cause of failure in the world of business and success is to quit, folk just give up, usually when the going gets tough, which it always will at some point.

So what is significant about, "In the beginning?"

Actually what I mean about in the beginning is to make sure you address the basics. Perhaps in the enthusiasm to "crack on" and get to the main part of our grand idea that leads us to forego sensible thinking and planning at the outset. Missing out the basics and coming unstuck in an effort to get to the success part a bit more rapidly. I am not really sure if there is one single reason, there probably isn't, but not dealing with the basics does cause a lot of problems later.

Would a rock performer turn up at the Hollywood Bowl with thousands of expensive tickets sold, but having no plan and never having rehearsed the show? Not likely. Busking isn't good enough, the ticket buyers would be rightly furious, yet sometimes entrepreneurs fail to plan and rehearse properly.

How do we begin? Simply, but not necessarily easily; in the beginning it is vitally important to develop a cohesive plan, usually built on a good idea. In nearly thirty years of running my own businesses and working with some very successful people I have been astonished how often people with a new business start-up focus on something further down the track instead of the first step; they're thinking and planning for the 100th. It's akin to a pilot considering his final approach before he has lined his aircraft up for take off.

Maybe the bullish pre match predictions by sports stars about the outcome, fools us into thinking preparation and hard work are not integral to the challenge. Or perhaps being misled is part of the human condition? Frankly I don't know.

What I am certain about however is that when Muhammad Ali confidently told reporters he would win his next fight in the fifth or the seventh round he had not somehow forgotten the rounds before, nor had he ignored the preparation and training needed. Far from it, he was very well prepared, he had thought through the whole thing, leading him to be able to predict when the fight would end with astonishing accuracy. Ali knew exactly what it took to win, he knew that planning to win in the fifth started with his training in the gym right at the beginning and by making sure he was well prepared. He was in effect goal setting.

Sometimes when setting up a first business or just thinking about doing it I come across people looking for a short cut, a silver bullet. I am never sure if it is impatience or maybe it is innate laziness. I suspect the reason does not matter, what does is the need to understand that success does require hard work and effort. There are no short cuts, no silver bullets.

The American motivational speaker Warren Greshes tells a wonderful story of a man who was unable to get a job as a janitor or caretaker at NYU, because he could not read or write. The man goes on to begin selling cigars on a street corner in the Wall Street area of New York. After many years of toil he discovers his supplier is looking to sell his store. Fed up with working in the rain and all kinds of weather he makes enquiries about buying the store. Resembling a down and out eventually he meets with a bank. He tells the manager at the bank all about his trials and tribulations, his inability to read or write and working all hours in all weathers.

The bank manager enquires about collateral or security, the man does not own any property, but does have money saved in the bank, so the bank manager looks the account up and discovers to his amazement the guy has saved hundreds of thousands Dollars and he asks the guy, "Do you know where you would be if you could read or write?"

The man answers as quick as a flash, "yeah I'd by the head janitor at NYU."

The moral of the tale? It is very simple of course, not only will nothing come to those who do nothing, but no matter your level of education or background, you can be successful. Hard work, the right attitude and taking the opportunities that present themselves is all that is required.

The object of this book is to provide some simple ideas, concepts and plans to help you make your business work and grow or turn your idea into a profitable enterprise. To do this I have drawn on my own experience, examples of situations my clients have faced and found solutions to, things that worked and things that did not. There are no magic formulas, no silver bullets. You have no need to have been born in the right place, have superhuman powers or to have gone to the right school.

Pre Match Warm Up

Whether you have a new ground breaking idea or simply want to make your own way in a more mature business, whatever your ambitions it is critical to have a plan. By this I don't mean a heavyweight tome or a one hundred page business plan (you might need one later if you need to raise funding), instead you require something more concise, more manageable. Something in fact, that will inspire and not intimidate you.

Sometimes it is possible to put a plan together that scares you so much you never set off on your journey.

Lots of successful people both in sport and business have said if they had known how tough it was going to be they may never have started, but they are so pleased they did. There are enough doubters in the world who will seek to derail you there is little sense undermining your own ambition.

Self-belief is a crucial aspect of success although some people are not naturally (or perhaps programmed through there up bringing) great self-believers. For them belief and confidence are built through having things work out. Making things happen. Conversely they feel insecure or their self-doubts are sadly reinforced if things don't work out. The fact is lots of things do not and will not work out. Those with self-belief just carry on regardless, to those looking from the outside it seems they never get anything wrong or make mistakes. That is utter nonsense of course. Everyone makes mistakes. The self-doubters need to find the courage to carry on. Persistence and tenacity are two critical factors in success.

Persistence means we just keep going and going until we succeed. Tenacity though is equally crucial, tenacity means we will look at what's not working and change it as we keep going.

If you are confident in the end goal is vital to be tenacious. Blindly persisting with the same thing is frankly nuts. It is worth remembering Albert Einstein's definition of insanity; *"..to keep repeating the same things expecting different results...."*

To begin any plan requires a few basic steps.

- What are you hoping to achieve ? What is your business?
- What does it provide? Who to?
- Why will they buy it or pay for your service?
- Have you got something unique?
- Does this disrupt, is it a new more efficient way of doing something that already exists?
- Is there a market for it?
- Is the market already saturated, can you compete?
- What resources do you need?
- Do you have the funding? If not, can you raise it?
- Do you need a licence, or other legal status to operate?
- Is what you do regulated by anyone?

Once you have all these points clearly set out, it pays to look at the financial aspects, even if your primary motive is not be the richest business owner ever, a business that cannot make a profit fails everyone. You will need to be realistic about the finances, how much can you sell your product for, how many times? What costs will there be to get to a sale of your product or service? Is the margin of profit sufficient to allow for reinvestment and development?

Clearly the most important facet of the beginning is to plan and plan well. But planning well does not mean complexity. The world is complex enough already.

Don't be put off if when you have looked at these issues if your idea suddenly looks less appealing. Ask yourself why that might be? Is there another way of achieving what you are seeking? Sometimes great ideas are not addressed to the right market, sometimes they are not the best idea at all. Either way, reflect on things and move on. Whatever you do, do not try to make the plan or the financials fit your idea because you are so in love with the idea that you cannot bear to let it go. Being too precious with your idea can be fatal.

One of the great attributes of successful people is making a decision to cull something they have created when it is no longer working and move on. Being overly sentimental can be dangerous and injurious to your wealth as well as your health.

There are occasions when it is possible to be completely blindsided by your own idea, especially if this happens to be something within an area that is very familiar, that you love or enjoy. For example seeking to turn a hobby into an enterprise, often we find ourselves surrounded by people with a similar love or enjoyment of the hobby. Raising your idea with them is frequently going to be met positively. They love their hobby too. However this does not mean there is a market, or not one which can be capitalised on profitably.

It is critical to make sure you consider the market opportunity for your idea. If there is no market, walk away, try again with something different. Do not try to bend your idea into a market.

Once you have the basics down it is also wise to spend a little time considering the competition. How do you stand up on the key issues of product specification, price, availability, reliability, delivery, distribution, geographic coverage, are there any unique selling points?

Armed with this you can now take a longer look at some crucial attributes required to turn your dream into reality. Does the plan look as good as your idea? If not, why not? Can you change it?

This harks back to my earlier remark about being in love with the idea, such that you become blindsided to the realities. Now is the ideal time to reassess this. If it looks sound on paper and that matches the sense in your head and heart then it is getting close to you being able to go for it.

A powerful yet simple thing to do now (some call it a trick, I prefer not to as the word trick implies a short cut, or a cheat. There are no short cuts..) is to think hard about what you want to achieve. Imagine the future as though you had already achieved it. Take your written goals and visualise your business in the future. Look at it, see what it brings.

See how your life has changed, look at every aspect of your life. We all love to day dream, so use this natural technique and hone it over time. The more you visualise your future, the better at it you will become. In turn the clearer the future will look for you. Your own mind becomes your greatest ally.

People often scoff at this idea, run it down even, describing it as hocus pocus; which is of course utter nonsense. There is a wonderful irony of those who scoff will also watch sport on television and eulogise about the performance or a particular sportsman or woman and marvel at their achievements, whilst conveniently overlooking the fact that sports people employ this technique and often openly talk about it.

Many years ago I watched a downhill ski race on television fascinated by the great Swiss skier Pirmin Zurbriggen's preparation. He was fully dressed to race, helmet and gloves on but standing off his skies leaning on his poles. With his eyes shut he began to ski the run in his mind, his hands out in front of him moving and turning with the slope. His head followed, all the way to the finish.

More recently Scottish tennis player Andy Murray became the first Briton to become the number one ranked tennis player in the world. In a brief excerpt from an interview he described how he had gone through visualising winning the point to win the game that would see him achieve his goal.

There must be countless other examples, if it is good enough for them it is good enough for you and me.

In addition to persistence and tenacity, there is a further vital ingredient to add to the mix, in a word commitment. It has been said that commitment is a little like virginity, you have either got it or you haven't.

How committed to your business are you? Are you really prepared for the hard work, stress, blood sweat and tears needed to succeed? If so and I have not put you off then welcome to the exciting world of doing your own thing, a world that opens up opportunity after opportunity.

One of the biggest challenges in new and small businesses is staying focused on the core objectives. As you set yourself free and work on your business plan you will suddenly find all sorts of other avenues opening before your eyes. The natural desire of many entrepreneurs is to try and grab all of them resulting in swamping yourself with too much to do and frequently meaning you dilute your results or worse find you never quite complete any one project and become disillusioned and give up.

Focus is another key requirement or starting and building a business. When I was young a phrase I often heard used was "shoemaker stick to thy last", roughly translated it means concentrate on what you are doing, or good at. Do not become side tracked, don't assume because things are proving more tricky than you had hoped that another opportunity or market for your product is somehow better or easier than where you are. The grass rarely is greener in these circumstances.

With focus on the core product, service and market comes mastery. Mastery means you have got to the stage where what you do is simplified, straightforward and possibly routine, this can be the clue to looking to scale your business, or grow to another stage. I will cover more of this in chapter five.

My own first business plan was very simple it ran to a page and a half of A4 paper! A type written document (no PC's or word processors then..), with an explanation of the idea, the market and how we were going to tackle the opportunity. It was supplemented with a hand drafted cashflow model.

Two years in the business was performing well, profitable and doing everything set out in the original plan. That began a process of reflection, with daily business going well, of course with a few ups, downs and some silly mistakes, it seemed now was the right time to expand, grow even. This was done somewhat off the cuff, little to no planning, confidence was high, fortunately on that occasion we got away with it. It is so very easy to forget the basics that got you to the stage where the possibility of expansion came into being. It is important to go back to the beginning, think through and plan appropriately.

About four years after the launch of the business with things going well, it seemed to be an ideal time to take another step and build further. Unlike the previous decision to grow this time we drew up a more comprehensive plan.

Even though the plan was more comprehensive, it was still fairly straightforward, despite this however a combination of over enthusiasm and over confidence caused the business to lurch a little which created a serious cashflow issue. Hard work, a helpful bank (yes they do exist) and commitment kept the whole thing going and back towards a path of growth. With that step established I became a lot more ambitious. The cause was the recognition that in an increasingly competitive environment, amidst ever evolving and complex regulation the business required even more scale not just to compete and grow but to survive.

On this occasion a more robust and complex business plan was developed the staffing levels of the business had increased substantially in the previous couple of years. Now for the first time the investment in people whose financial return to the business was likely to be several years out and with it of course a large increase in the risk levels.

There were so many financial projections the UK Treasury would have been proud of it. But it was all meaningless drivel. Nevertheless on we went and consequently nearly ruined everything. It was the root cause of me and my then colleagues going our separate ways and me starting again.

The extraordinary irony was that the idea, the guts of the plan was right, it was the execution that was terrible.

After a period of fighting and scraping my way through I did eventually put that plan into practice. I am pleased to say it worked and continues to work. The solution frankly was just to get on with it, things were far from perfect the timescale to achieve the goals extended. By just getting on with it and testing ideas, improving what worked and ditching what doesn't it is perfectly feasible to get yourself into a position of relative strength without the need to produce a mega business plan of unbelievable sophistication. It might intrigue the bank, or be greeted with enthusiasm by the Venture Capital funders in the City of London but it is just as often likely to be a hindrance as it is a help.

Very early in my business career I was told there are three stages to success;

1. Youthful enthusiasm.
2. Complicated sophistication.
3. Mature simplicity.

I believed this, so much so I was determined to miss the second one out, sadly I did not. I feel fortunate to have survived having fallen into the trap. I have met many others who have taken the same path, so many of those who got hung up by complicated sophistication quit and either found a way to create a lifestyle business or they have gone on to find a job. Some years later they still harbour regrets; occasionally I even meet someone quite bitter because of the experience. Don't let that be you.

Good ideas make good businesses, sometimes there is almost no such thing as a bad idea. Sometimes it is worth taking ideas and testing them by seeing if they sell, do it small, don't go mad, then either refine and develop or ditch the idea. Either way do it as quickly as you can. Do not fall in love with the idea, if it's not working stop.

Some ideas are worth parking and maybe returning to when the time is right. One word of warning, be careful about trendy new business ideas.

Today there is an app for everything and for every app there are hundreds and sometimes thousands more. Some of them are really great, some not so good at all, much like anything in life.

Somehow with the age of the internet and Steve Zuckerberg for inspiration it seems to me that half the bright young things in the UK think they can and will make their fortune from a new app. Some probably will. Most won't.

Why is this?

Some of the fundamentals of business life are the same today as they have always been. The mistaken view that it is different this time seems as unshakeable in people's minds as I have ever known. Several times a year I meet or speak to a bright software developer who has a new app or gaming idea. Usually the conversation is about them raising funds or organising bank debt.

They also become quite despondent when I explain to them the difficulties of attracting funding in a market where new ideas and proposals are being viewed by funders at quite staggering rates. I am close to one source of capital that receives 20 new proposals a week; now that would not be many if they had a large team however they are a team of three people! Frankly to get past the first approach you need one heck of an elevator pitch. Another larger venture firm I know well sees about 3,000 proposals a year, they back fewer than twenty.

Despondency gives way quickly to annoyance, some even saying, "It's not like it was in your day, things are different now. Everyone uses an app for their life."

Of course they are right, but they are also quite wrong. They are right that app's are now an integral part of most people's daily life in the developed world, but wrong that business is different today. What they rarely recognise is the staggering array of app's and games available, many of them free, provided to download in the hope the downloader will then buy something subsequently.

A funder will want to see a little more than a two page business plan exclaiming the virtues of the designers app or game. They will seek some validation of the product or service, in other words proof of your concept. In addition they may want evidence that shows it not only does what you claim, but does so commercially. There has to be a ready and viable market for it. Funding very early stage, pre revenue ideas requires both a lot of faith and deep pockets in order to fund the development, followed by hundreds of thousands of free downloads in the hope of a sale at the end of the line. To get to this point you must be as credible as your business idea.

At a business level it is no different today than in times gone by. Recently in a bid to explain this to someone I came up with the following analogy.

"The problem for app and game designers is the same as the person who goes into a quality restaurant. They see the fancy plate of food, the appetising ballotine of chicken with a fancy mushroom foam on the side. When you taste the foam there is a wonderful deep taste of mushroom, the experience is extraordinary. On the one hand you are eating something that looks like bubble bath but on the other it tastes like freshly harvested mushrooms. What they fail to see is how the food got there."

Firstly someone had to find and pick the mushrooms; they needed transporting to the restaurant, cleaning and cooking before it could be turned into foam. New cooking techniques provided by technology allow the mushrooms to be turned into foam, but everything else that happened was the same as it was 100 years ago, nothing new at all.

If your business or business plan is all about foam and ignores the fundamentals then expect to find funders saying no.

If you have the money yourself and press on be sure there is a market for foam and people prepared to pay for it. By thoroughly thinking through what you are going to do, make or sell you may well discover the best thing to do is start with just mushrooms and add the foam version later. Learning to walk first is as true now as it ever was.

Among many business clients I have worked with over the last few years a couple have seen me helping them in looking for a business to buy. One of the most extraordinary things that has become evident is the number of businesses, probably the majority that have no settled means of selling their product or service. No matter how good your product or service, if it relies exclusively on the inventor or creator to gather sales as well then the business will inevitably stall or worse.

Another challenge which crops up on a regular basis is for the founder of the business who recognises the need for a sales function has been the major difficulty they have in recruiting the right people.

Sales skills are often viewed as being natural attributes of an individual with an outgoing personality. Or sometimes are looked down on by very creative technicians, almost dismissively. Selling is in fact a difficult skill, for any business to truly succeed it is an essential skill. It is not an easy skill to acquire. Frequent failure and rejection waits around every corner even for the most proficient and successful sales people.

Dealing with rejection in this way is trying, but necessary if you are to survive. Great football strikers miss more attempts on goal than they score, so it is with sales.

It is beyond the scope of this short book to go into the skills needed, the methods of acquiring them and honing them. However one simple thought to log and put into practice is to focus on your prospects need and desired outcome. Fully understanding this and what's in it for them is the key to getting a fruitful relationship going.

By demonstrating to the prospect that the relationship is going to be about them is essential. I have always loved the following quote by Theodore Roosevelt;

"Nobody cares how much you know until they know how much you care."

KICK OFF

Now you're ready to take the next step, hopefully when you get here your heart is racing a little as the excitement builds. Impatience maybe getting the better of you and I know from my own experience reigning it in can be quite a challenge! But keeping control is important.

In a way this chapter could be very short, maybe summarised with *"just get going"*. However whilst it is true to say that all long journey's start with the first small step there are a few things that need to be considered beforehand. After all you would not step straight into the road without checking the traffic would you?

At its most basic this is checking that you have everything. Your business plan, premises if you need them, equipment, staff, all the legal documents you might need, your bank and accountants all organised.

Have you got the correct operating structure you need, whether that is a Limited company or Limited Liability Partnership?

Set yourself a start date then get on with it.

Like your car though you cannot just run it and ignore the mechanics, the moving parts. Your business will need fuel, oil and water on a regular basis. The engine will need to be serviced the electronics and instruments checked. Failure to do this will run the risk of a breakdown or worse.

What in the context of your business does this mean?

Firstly your business plan needs to be broken down to simpler small parts again. To monitor how you are progressing against your plan it is helpful to set specific smaller and measurable goals. This becomes your business instrument panel, just like the car. By, setting measurable goals together with timescales to achieve your goals you can get constant feedback on progress. In corporate speak you will often see this referred to as key performance indicators or KPI's. Whatever you choose to call them they should be written down and visited regularly.

- Pearson's Law, "That which is measured improves. That which is measured and reported improves exponentially." Karl Pearson

They should become part of your ongoing strategy, as you review and reflect on them you may need or want to revise them, for example if you are ahead of your revenue target at the half year, should you consider increasing it?

Set your written goals out in a method that works best for you. Do not set too many and make sure they reflect the plan. Then as I have already stated you need to review them regularly. I look at my own weekly and monthly with a quarterly review where I record progress and if the goal is achieved set a new one. If it is not, then you need to ask why? Do we need to change something, replace a broken part? Have we set the wrong goal or made another error that can be rectified. If something is outside your control do not fret about it, move on.

It may seem odd, but if you are ahead of target, ask yourself why before resetting. Was the cause a one off exceptional item or some other freakish event that might not be repeatable? If so then review the progress to your target missing this exceptional item out. It is very easy to wind up misleading yourself and then find the new revised goal is missed and beat yourself up as a result. Worse if you have outside funders or backers and you reset things but do not achieve them they may see the second period as a failure and you risk more applied pressure. It is amazing how short memories can be. Pressure you really will not need.

Measurement of your progress is vital, firstly we respond well to seeing how we have done. This is particularly so when measuring against where we came from or checking how much we have improved. I must commend one man's writing and thoughts here, indeed the man responsible for pointing this out to me. Dan Sullivan of Strategic Coach wrote a short but powerful book called "Mind the Gap." In it he addresses the tendency to measure ourselves against a goal we set but did not quite reach or of measuring ourselves against others. He champions the idea of comparing just how far we have come or how much progress we have made from the past. "The Gap" is the distance between where we are and perhaps the progress of others or that goal we did not quite get to. Falling in the gap can be very disheartening and of course can lead to our confidence falling.

Measurement can teach us all kinds of things about our business, whether that might be about our marketing or sales strategy and what is working and what is not. If you are responsible for sales are you having the right number of meetings? Seeing the right number of new prospects or just having cosy discussions with existing customers? You must be honest with yourself when doing this.

If you don't like what you learn from the answers please do not become despondent. Discovering you might not be going about something the right way is a positive thing as it will help you to refocus and make sure you are dealing with the right things. Occasionally if progress has not been as you would have wished then finding out you have been going about something in a less effective manner than you would like, can once you have planned to change, provide a huge boost of energy.

It is far too simple to conclude you are the problem, when it might be the approach.

Thirty years ago golfer Sir Nick Faldo changed coach and with that change they changed his swing completely. At the time he was a regular winner on tour and was considered to be one of the most talented younger players on the European tour, but in his view not quite doing well enough.

Some thought the actions he took under his new coach David Leadbetter to be extreme, too great a risk, but within a couple of years he went from major championship outsider to multiple major championship winner and the number one ranked player in the world. Small adjustments can sometimes produce profound results.

Another way to think of this is small adjustments to your heading if you were steering a ship across the ocean and you were a tiny fraction of a degree out instead of reaching say New York you might arrive in the Caribbean. Imagine where the NASA rockets would have ended up if after lift off the crew had maintained a fraction of a degree inaccuracy in their heading!

Monitor, check and adjust are fundamental to any business success. Not a sign of failure.

Sadly it's when looking at the progress that falls short of expectations that some people give up, often wrongly assuming they got it all wrong and failed.

SUSTAIN THE EFFORT

As the initial enthusiasm begins to wane particularly when the enterprise runs into inevitable roadblocks it is ever more vital to stick to the basics of your plan and keep with it. The temptation to quit can become quite powerful, this testing time for any entrepreneur is when you need to dig deep and stick with it. Winston Churchill once said "Keep buggering on" or another gem of his I like "When you are going through hell, keep going."

Olympic gold medal winning swimmer Adam Peaty actually listens to Churchill's speeches on his i Pod or i Phone before he competes.

Churchill's words are merely another way of highlighting the need to be persistent. To the outside observer some business successes seem to be miraculous, an overnight achievement that must have been the result of a magic formula others do not possess. Whilst some businesses have enjoyed a meteoric rise most that do develop in this way frequently end up being like a meteor or comet which eventually burn up and crash. Very few are sustainable.

The reality is a lot of businesses which appear to be overnight successes will often have had a particular tipping point, that brought success. Looking on from the outside it is hard to see the many trials and tribulations and years of effort put into making the business work, by the founders, before they reached that tipping point.

Keeping your head up and keeping going when everything seems futile or lost is an essential ingredient in the recipe of business success. The measurement of progress, monitoring goals and making the requisite adjustments I referred to in the previous chapter are vital to sustaining your plan.

Part of the process of monitoring the health of your business is also the management of your resources, especially your human resources. My business career has mostly been in financial services. Over the years I have seen and known many who regard employees as a necessary evil or worse an expense that they will do everything possible to avoid. Others however have taken the view that getting the right people on board is an invaluable investment in the future of their business and the catalyst for the business becoming self sustaining.

The object of course is to create an enterprise that does not require you to be working in it all day everyday, but affords you the time to work on the business, developing, moulding and growing the enterprise. Rather like a sculpture.

Those that see employees as a cost are in effect not running a business at all they are merely operating and sustaining a job. No one who succeeds does so alone. The stronger the team around you the greater are the chances of your success.

I am sure you must have heard people say (maybe you have even said it yourself, I confess I have in the past...) in frustration or exasperation, *"If you want something doing, you might as well do it yourself."*

Could this be because you do not have the right people on your team? Or maybe you gave a task to someone without the requisite skills or knowledge to carry it out? If so it's not their fault it's yours.

Sometimes we make recruitment mistakes, occasionally though we ask things of others they are not equipped to do and on those occasions it is important to consider the level of investment you are making in training.

- Goalkeepers keep goal, strikers score them, it is best not to change roles or try to convert one into the other.

Perhaps you need a resource or skill on an infrequent basis? If so consider outsourcing the task. I have done this often only seeking to employ someone full time when the demand for capacity justified the investment.

To some outsourcing is a bad idea and in truth it can be tricky getting the right partner to work with. However outsourcing is something you can turn on or off which enables you to have greater control of costs, clearly it is often much easier than hiring for a role. One other challenge for a small growing enterprise is the need to solve multiple problems and find demand in your business grows in a different area and the person you hired is not the right person for that area even with the input of training and the associated expense; not to mention the additional time needed. Not that I am suggesting you should avoid investing in training and development. Quite the opposite however like any additional investment it is better if it can be planned and if the need you have in the business is relatively short term then outsourcing or bringing in a specialist temporary resource makes more sense.

These are the sorts of capacity challenges most early stage businesses struggle with. Consequently the founder ends up doing it themselves, the result being they are back to working in the business and not on it, probably putting in 18 hour days seven days a week. The level of fatigue this will bring if the effort continues for too long will result in the business struggling elsewhere or health issues.

Capacity challenges like this can occur through greed, or maybe desperation to get new business after a fallow period, so the business owner takes on more work than the enterprise has capacity to cover. The temptation to take too much on is obvious. It might be possible to get away with this occasionally but as a business strategy it is plain stupid. At best it leads to relationship issues with customers, clients, suppliers and staff and at worst loss from some or all of these.

It strikes me that people view outsourcing from the wrong perspective. Consider for a moment, would you provide your own legal advice (even if you are a lawyer)? Chances are you would not, you would take advice, in other words you buy in the service. In effect you outsource the task.

Sometimes finding the right relationship to outsource can prove challenging. I had one such issue a few years ago. I had "plugged" a few gaps in my team with part time employees. It worked well for all, I had people good at their roles who only wanted to work a limited number of hours and I had insufficient capacity in each role for them to be full time hires.

As business began to progress however I was challenged to try to find more part timers, recruit a full time person or identify work we could outsource. The problem grew over about a 12 month period to the point where it was in danger of getting out of hand. Things became worse when one of my part time team, who had joined two years earlier having left his permanent job came to me and said he wanted to move to full time retirement.

The solution we came up with had two stages, the first was to outsource different elements of client work where we could find the right support. The second was to sell part of the business.

As anyone who has bought or sold a business will tell you the second part of my plan was not a quick thing. All in all the process took over 18 months. For a further two years after selling I was beginning to wonder if I had made a catastrophic error, after all we not only lost the income from the existing business but a valuable source of introduced word of mouth work. My plan was simply to shrink the business to grow it by refocussing on what we are best at and our preferred target market.

Although the first period immediately after the sale was challenging, the plan has worked, what's more I have found it much easier to recruit the right people into key roles. As the business has been growing and profits have recovered the value of the business is now greater than before the sale. The sustainability of the income has improved exponentially and as we have been able to focus and spend more time working on the business so we have also seen a sharp up turn in new business. Shrink to grow can be made to work.

No business is still for long, so if you are not constantly working on "it" then the business will take a direction all of its own and sometimes the business owner does not spot the problem until it is either too late or the requirements to change become almost unmanageable.

Put bluntly your business will only ever be as successful as the quality of the team you build, whether in house or outsourced or both.

The quality of the team around you then is the essential building block of the business. Have you noticed how many web sites proclaim that the most valuable asset the company has is its people? For me not only is this actually the case, but it must be seen to be the case.

Frequently when I visit company's it is most definitely not the case and many not only pay lip service to the fact but they use weird slogans and days or nights out in a bid to be seen to care and value the team. This might seem like I am being rude or even abusive towards some entrepreneurs. It is not my intent, but it is critical that you look after your people, it is after all they who will interface with your customers or clients often more so than you. If your customer is the most important person you deal with then doesn't it follow that the people who look after them are equally important?

What does treating them as valued actually mean?

Clearly it goes without saying they should be as well paid as can be achieved, they should be incentivised and again when and where possible receive additional benefits. But more than this they should be treated as valued in the more subtle and day to day manner than is often the case. To me this means treated with respect, being polite and seen as equals. Genuinely involving them in the wider thinking of the business, not just in their roles, how you address them in public and in front of each other can have a surprising impact on the way you are viewed.

If it is necessary to deal with issues of discipline then do it in private, but again with respect, be polite. Just as important is to praise in public, try to avoid doing so in private. Share information with your team, for example the finances, if they understand the impact of costs on the bottom line is it not more likely your people will seek to avoid waste and reduce costs where they can?

Do the non sales people in your organisation really appreciate the value of the top line? Do the sales people understand the need for margin and not just sales at any price? You will be amazed at how many organisations do not seem to have that covered and this is not exclusive to small businesses or start- ups, larger mature and sometimes publicly quoted companies of long standing lose sight and fall into the same trap.

Another way to look at your organisation and focus minds is to consider the hierarchy. Would it be fair to say that most company organisation charts have the CEO and the board at the top? Thereafter, typically several layers of people before the members of the team that deal with the customers most regularly. Frankly this makes no sense for a lot of enterprises, because it's the wrong way around! Especially, where customer service is a large part of what you do.

Try turning your organisation chart on its head. Put the customer at the top, next the people who deal with the customer. Then those who deal with these people and so on. Whether you are a manufacturer, service organisation or a tech company you are but nothing without satisfied customers, people who spend money on what you have to offer, the upside down organisation chart focuses your teams attention on this.

Moreover if you back this with permission to resolve the customer's needs (within reason of course and not at any price), your team will be properly engaged in what matters. Any organisation that operates in the traditional form will by definition be less successful at customer service.

Recently I was contacted by email concerning my car's pending third birthday, with the offer of a "packaged" service and check which was to include the cars first MOT. As I intend to keep the car I booked it in for the offered service.

The service was completed and I collected my car at the end of the day and gave the matter no further thought for about a week, when I suddenly realised I had not been provided with an MOT certificate. So I rang to query this and was told that since the car was not exactly three years old at the time of the service they had not carried out the MOT test. However the day I rang back it was three years old and of course requires an MOT certificate. I raised the fact that the MOT was included in the package and referred to the email and the date it was sent to the customer service person. The company apologised and I was told there would be no charge for the MOT, which I was pleased about especially as I now had to make the trip to the garage again at my cost of both fuel and time, so we booked the car in for its MOT the following week.

As a courtesy the garage called me the day before to remind me of the appointment. So far so good. Then things started to go all big corporate, as we were ending the call the very polite person on the phone then asked me if I had the email to which I had referred to when calling them to point out the error? Fortunately it was in my deleted items so when I was as asked I was able to forward it to them.

On the face of it, perhaps it was not unreasonable for them to check I was not trying to get one over on them, but, I had actually given them the date and the name of the sender of the email containing the offer so a simple check their end should have sufficed, or at least that is what I thought. The reason I was being asked however is because the customer services person was being obliged to demonstrate the reason for booking in a no cost MOT to their line manager. The company clearly provides little or no capacity for the customer service people to resolve issues.

This was hardly a critical issue for me, but it is a simple example of customer service loose ends that need not exist, a decent CRM system would clearly be a start, something you might think a major global brand could afford, but there is also an issue of management. Organisations that empower their people to resolve matters for customers and encourage their people to grow and develop tend also to get better customer response and feedback than those who do not.

Clearly it is important to be reasonable with the delegation of responsibility, in the end the entrepreneur is responsible, but by making sure that permission to resolve customer issues rests with the people dealing with your customer and does not need to be referred back up the line on each occasion will ensure much less of the entrepreneurs time is used resolving issues. This saves money, improves the image of the organisation with the customer who in turn is more likely to be an advocate for you than if the matter has to go around the houses endlessly before being sorted. The focus on this will save money and feed straight to the bottom line. A good maxim to remember is turnover is vanity, profit is sanity.

If your team understand what is needed to make things profitable and the relationship of profit to their salary then sleeves get rolled up and the effort is made to ensure the business is a success. Believe me they will dig in and make sure they work with you to get out of any hiccups.

No man is an island

As you move through your business life it is essential to take stock on a regular basis and stand back from the day to day. Maybe when you started you took some advice, or received guidance from a coach or one of the many Government sponsored business hubs. There is in fact a whole plethora of resource available, including books, online sites, business consultants and coaching services.

One surprising thing I find is the number of business owner entrepreneurs who took advice at the beginning to help with start up only to stop once things had got off the ground. I use a coach and whilst not always the same one I have used them for many years.

At an event in London recently I was sitting next to a guy who was in the relatively early stages of his business and finding himself struggling to cope. He was working harder than ever and making little to no progress. He could see no way out of his situation other than running harder.

The day was a "pitch" event organised by the The Strategic Coach, which is the coaching service I use; as a client I was able to attend the day. The morning was dedicated to the pitch with a short but helpful session as part of the pitch which was equally helpful to existing clients such as me. The session was simple in so much as it afforded the audience an opportunity to think through a concept aimed at helping entrepreneurs ensure they could devote time to working on and not in their business. It was backed up with evidence of how this had worked on multiple occasions, furthermore in the room were plenty of people who had been working with the coach over a number of years who could support the claims.

Anyone new signing on for the service was able to attend the afternoon workshop. There were business people in the room not only from the UK but who had flown in from overseas one had even come from Australia.

At the end of the session I asked the guy what he thought. He had enjoyed the morning and got a good deal from it, but felt he could not commit to signing up. He was too busy and had to get to his office to make sure he was ready for a meeting the following day. What irony given that the presentation and concept run through had been designed to help with this very problem!

I suspect he will not sign up subsequently and worse might not use anyone else. The outcome being that he will just have to run harder and harder. Frequently the only way to make progress and achieve the next breakthrough business is to identify ways to work smarter not harder. Working harder usually means doing the same thing repeatedly over longer and longer hours. Remember Einstein's definition of insanity? This is a perfect example.

Beyond my daily business life I am lucky to have had a fair deal of experience in elite sport (not as a participant you understand), via my wife's equestrian career. She is also a coach and trainer of others. I am not sure if it is a peculiar British disease or merely a human failing, but I regularly see new pupils come to her for help with their horses, many will make rapid progress with their objectives and after a few short sessions stop. When asked why they stopped the response normally being they have learned the one thing they set out to achieve, they have "made it." Sport provides a great opportunity for quick feedback and more often than not those that decide they have learned all they can or do not need any further help start to see their results going backwards after they have given up on coaching. The most common reaction to this situation is the rider thinks through their issues trying to recall the training they had received and attempt to implement their recollections, only to find things get worse still.

The cause of the double dip, is simple, firstly giving up on coaching to begin with and then inaccurately recalling the training and implementing (in ignorance) bad practice.

There is no doubt that taking on a coach or business adviser can be uncomfortable, there is an outlay and it might take some time to recoup the cost. Sometimes finding the time and money is challenging, particularly if you are doing the job of several people. But somewhere along the line the change will occur. You have a choice of either being in control of when and how, or you wait until your health gives in or your business runs into difficulties when it might prove even harder to solve the challenges you face.

- My advice is get "guru – ed" up.

What this means is to make sure you find and use either an advisor, mentor or coach. You may even need two at the same time. At various times I have used all three and two at the same time. For example a specialist advisor in marketing who helped me better define my business process so that we could sharpen our marketing messages, whilst also using a business coach.

Some years ago I used a mentor, we would meet every quarter and he essentially acted as an external conscious, checking and monitoring my key performance indicators with me. Making sure I did not fall short of being honest with myself. When I thanked him for his time, he would frequently say, "I have done nothing, all I do is hold a mirror up for you to look in." Sometimes the answer to our problems is closer to hand than we realise and the external stimulus can be all that is needed to focus our minds. In turn over the last ten years I have performed this role with others. I get a great deal of satisfaction from it and I also learn a tremendous amount from this activity.

One personal fault of mine is to be too hard on myself. This is not something I alone suffer from, so I recommend you take care in how you approach personal honesty. There is a fine balance to strike between making sure you are honest with yourself and beating yourself up. Outside help can help get this balance right.

It may appear as though I am labouring this point rather, however being honest with yourself is a crucial part of measuring your progress, which in turn is key to your future success. It will also help you manage and avoid unnecessary risk. Measurement can act as an early warning system, just like an airline pilots instruments. Throughout a flight a pilot will keep a constant check on the "T's and P's" or temperatures and pressures. Crucial gauges in ensuring the aircrafts engines are performing as required. So it is with business. By measuring progress you can highlight problems which need to be addressed or spot opportunities that can be capitalised upon. So I make no apology for being repetitive.

The outside influence of an advisor, coach or mentor can really help in making sure this is successful.

Scoring Goals

All businesses experience cycles, some of course are more prone to cyclicality than others, particularly things that are sensitive to the overall economic situation, for example Oil & Gas businesses tends to suffer if the overall economic outlook weakens and they are in the vanguard of growth when economic activity accelerates. Other business such as food and consumer staples are of course much less volatile as they produce and sell things people will buy regardless of whether an economy is growing or contracting.

Understanding where your business fits in the cyclical nature of the economy can be very helpful and potentially crucial to both survival and success. Although the statistics can be misleading and perhaps hide a few mitigating factors it is never the less true that more businesses struggle to survive or even fail in the early years than succeed. According to a survey conducted by the UK insurer Royal Sun Alliance (RSA) fewer than 50% of start ups since the financial crisis have survived for more than 5 years. The survey cites many reasons, from lack of available funding to red tape and tax and much more besides. In my experience there are some very simple things that go wrong, having been on the wrong side of one of these more than once, but lived to tell the tale! What are they?

Cashflow

It might sound obvious, but without the wherewithal to pay the bills you are sunk. Some early stage enterprises get in a mess with cashflow because of poor planning. Over optimistic projections (be honest with yourself) for business growth, margin and sales. Mispricing your product or under estimating the cost of production, sales and marketing can all create cashflow challenges.

Or maybe no one wants what you are selling – remember my earlier remarks about proof of concept and testing.

Poor sales and marketing – customers will not simply turn up to buy from you because you have opened the door. You have to tell them about yourself, entice them in get them to look at what you are offering. Not every great creator is a born salesman or marketeer.

Maladministration

This can of course lead to cashflow issues if you don't get invoices out and paid on time. But poor business administration skills can lead to all kinds of challenges. These tend to be the sorts of things business owners can get to grips with fairly quickly even if they are not the core skills of the enterprises founder. But it is better to plan for them at the start than have them distract you at a crucial time. Many infuriating aspects of Government red tape can go unresolved or even ignored if the back office does not function correctly, any of which could cause your business to fail or be closed down if you breach a regulation or the law, however inadvertent that might be. The publicity fallout can be disastrous even if you do manage to survive the initial problem.

Trying to do everything yourself – this can be caused by cashflow, or worries about cashflow – is unwise at best and foolhardy at worst. The consequences for you personally and the business can be awful. The temptation is of course obvious, the business is yours and no one else cares as much as you, no one else can do the job as well as you right?

Wrong!

Despite what we might think it is not the case that we are best at everything frequently someone else will be better at certain things than you. Having the right people on the team is crucial as I said in the last chapter.

Staffing

Businesses that are not growing will all too often be stagnating. Seeking business growth is not about greed it is in fact fundamental to surviving.

Growth can come in different forms, it does not have to be linear growth in turnover, and whilst this is appealing growth in turnover with shrinking profit margins is as much use as a chocolate teapot unless somewhere down the line you can re-grow the margin.

Some businesses can be sustained by growing recurring revenue as part of turnover but the top line number might not be advancing very much. Increased recurring revenue has two great attributes; predictable cashflow brings security and the ability to plan for the business more efficiently. Secondly it will increase the value of the enterprise if you were seeking a potential fund raising or outright sale. The business will be more attractive to a buyer or investor.

Growing revenue is an exciting thing to do. If your business has reached a stage where the people in place can manage and run the enterprise with limited involvement from the entrepreneur you get to start all over again. This time with the financial security of revenue behind you and of course proof that you can do it, with that evidence your confidence is far higher than it might have been at other times. At this point if you are seeking to grow the business by adding services or manufacturing something else then you must go right back to the beginning and follow all the steps as though it were a start-up, with one added question. Will this distract us from what we do, will it add value?

Success and growth can of course provide lots of new challenges, some of them not even the best entrepreneurs can solve indeed they can often be the worst people to try to solve them. Just as not everyone is cut out to be an entrepreneur so not everyone is cut out to be a great administrator of a business, overseeing its day to day operations, managing the issues that arise, staffing, finances and the myriad of complexity that comes with success and scale. Whilst you may have had to do everything yourself at the beginning there comes a point when you cannot and in order to move forwards others need to join you. Failure to recognise this can be a disaster for a business. However embracing it and making sure you identify the talents needed to fill the roles created will help free you from the burden of managing the business. With this freedom you will find the opportunity to expand and grow further as you bring more new and fresh ideas to the business.

Once you have the right team you must embrace them, bring them into the core of the enterprise. The old days of "us and them" are long since dead. Collaborative work with colleagues will foster far more benefit than the cost of the extra overhead. Remember the right team is an investment and the very heartbeat of your business.

Making sure all the team are pulling together and share the values of the enterprise can be of greatest benefit, particularly when the company faces challenges. Going through difficult times is part of life, it's unpleasant but not totally avoidable there is a wonderful saying worth remembering when thinking about your team "people don't sink the boat they are sailing in."

Of course finding the right people is not always as easy as it sounds. It is also possible that you can make the wrong hire or put someone into a role they are not best suited for, that of itself is sometimes enough to prevent entrepreneurs even trying. Although these situations can be challenging, it is a mistake to not to persevere in search of the right team.

I know one entrepreneur well who has built a substantial operation that has become far too big for him to manage. To begin with he broke the business into a couple of separate units, the more established of the two he left to his team to run with only a small amount of his time being spent on oversight each week. They had a straightforward process for winning new business, which was as close to turnkey as he could manage so the amount of time he was required to spend within it was not excessive. In effect the position he was in was much like a ship's Captain who is not at the helm all the time, but has a trusted crew to keep steering the ship in the right direction. However also like the ship's Captain all of the big decisions needed his input and as the business continued to grow in turn it increased the amount of time he had to spend working in this side of the enterprise.

The effect of this was to bring him almost back to square one and the other side of the business was now getting less input and not making the progress he was seeking. The solution was to employ a Chief Executive. This proved challenging, the first two did not work out, but the principle was right so he stuck at it and the third incumbent has made a success of the role, freeing his time to take the new smaller side of the business forward to the next level. Knowing him as I do I have little doubt this will also be a great success. Even proven successful entrepreneurs run into difficulty in this area of development.

Funding

Growing businesses can sometimes need additional funding, the source and type required rather depends on what the growth entails and the long term objectives of the business and the entrepreneur. The need can vary, it could be to add staff, which although expensive they are but nothing compared to some types of product development (of course this may require extra human capital also) or manufacturing development or perhaps applying for global patents. The latter can be an enormous financial burden, but if what you have is unique then protecting your rights to that product may be key to your long term survival and of course the rewards that go with the risks and endeavour.

If your business is small the first thing to look at is your own cashflow. Can you add the person or persons needed from existing cashflow? This might mean restricting your own reward but if you believe in your business then this will pay dividends in time, after all people are an investment not a cost.

If you cannot manage it this way, have you got savings or other capital you can introduce to the business? If so then probably lending the money to your own business is the most efficient way to do this.

If this is not possible can you turn to your bank for help? A simple overdraft might suffice, clearly by going down this road you will need to present the bank with some sort of business and financial plan that includes not only a cashflow model but a forecast profit and loss, all of which needs to be supported by past financial data, such as audited accounts, if you have them. If not then the quality of your presentation and business case will need to be top notch.

Without evidence to support the business case the bank will need to be convinced by you, do they believe in you, can they trust you to deliver?

They may also seek some sort of security if you are able to provide this. If you can offer security a bank is more likely to be able to lend over a longer period for example a five year period. This is cheaper than an overdraft, as it has a fixed monthly schedule of payment and is easier to budget for. However if you do not need all of the funds at once then an overdraft could be the lower cost option. The cost of debt is also materially affected by security, clearly if the lender can seek to secure its loan then the cost of the debt is very likely to be lower than if the debt is unsecured.

Sometimes security is not possible if you are in this position can your family or friends help you, what are you prepared to give them in return?

When writing your business plan I recommend you write it to cover five years and have financial forecasts that cover each year. At the very least it needs to extend to three years.

Your cashflow forecasts will tell you when you can expect to make repayment of any debt. As with the initial plan make sure you are honest with yourself, be realistic and conservative with your forecasting. It is worth living by a simple motto here, "promise long and deliver short", this applies equally to sales and promises you make to customers or clients. What I mean by this is best explained with a simple example; if you expect something to take 3 weeks to complete normally but you might deliver in 2 weeks, then suggesting to your customer, client or bank that it will take 4 weeks and delivering in under 3 weeks will earn you considerable kudos.

Clearly with using the bank there is a balance to strike as if the time taken would actually run to months or years, having too long to the final repayment may put them off. The flip side is by making a promise of a tight timescale and then falling short will not help you. If this is something that is causing you issues to resolve or decide then seeking help or advice from someone who has "been and gone and done it" can be invaluable, or perhaps your accountant can help you think the plans through. In the UK there are also Government sponsored services available which include regional Business Growth Hubs with a variety of resources in place, a helpful Government website can be found at www. greatbusiness.gov.uk. In the USA there are also various regional, State level and national resources, a good place to start is https://www.sba. gov/starting-business.

Over recent years there has been an enormous growth in alternative forms of lending from investment funds specialising in providing debt, private equity style firms specialising in non equity funding, peer to peer lending and now an increasing number of challenger banks.

An alternative to traditional bank finance is factoring or invoice discounting. Today there are many specialist providers in this field who can help. However that help can be pricey but is a very effective way of guaranteeing invoices get paid in a timely manner removing some of the cashflow risk that can kill a business.

If you either cannot get the funds or you establish in your own mind that it is not possible to start your new plan or project at this stage then you might either need to scale the plan back a little such that it does work, or delay starting until you are in better shape. As part of this exercise be clear about what you are seeking to do;

- What am I seeking to achieve?
- What do I need to know to progress?
- What resources, human, financial or otherwise do I need?
- What does success look like?

Depending upon the scale of business or opportunity you might of course need to consider getting external capital into your business. This could involve specialist venture capital partners, private equity firms or other investors such as business angels. The price is the equity you relinquish and of course the likelihood that any investor may want a presence on your board. There is a positive flip side to this as the right investor could also provide you with the skills and expertise to accomplish your goals. Having a smaller share of a bigger pie may prove to be a lot more rewarding than one hundred percent of a tiny pie.

Finding the right venture partner however can be tortuous. For many years now I have worked with clients in this area and it is far from easy and it is quite understandable that some business owners seek to stay as they are, or grow more slowly under their own steam using only their own resources. For some businesses this is simply not possible, either because they have a massively capital intensive operation such as manufacturing or a business seeking to capitalise on an opportunity that competitors are likely to be considering or has some kind of time sensitivity attached to the opportunity. In these cases outside funding is always likely to be the best source. It is worth remembering that the stronger your business case the less equity you will have to let go.

Some funders will look to split their funding between debt and equity, the former gives them an immediate cash return on their investment and the equity is their risk involvement. Depending on your circumstances this can be positive or negative to you, so think carefully before committing. Having more than one offer is of course a desirable position if you can make this happen.

In the life of any business there will come a point where growth causes major headaches. Growing pains are normal, but they can also be very challenging and damaging if not managed correctly. I have already mentioned in the chapter "Sustain the Effort" the need to manage capacity issues. It is very easy to get this wrong, the likelihood of perfection is improbable, accept that you will make mistakes. What will matter is not so much whether or not you do make any errors, but what you do about them when they arise.

Typical growing pain challenges can be taking on more new business than you have the capacity to manage, this can lead to disappointed customers or clients and of course a loss of business. If this starts to get out of hand it is very tempting to cut the margins and reduce costs to your customers. Frankly this is nuts. Trying to deliver the service that you are already struggling with for less money is unlikely to end well.

Sometimes these challenges in a small business can draw all the team into handling the work for the customer. This can cause things like bill payment to suffer as no one is keeping an eye on when invoices are being settled, or worse not even sending them in the first place. Costs can start to drift as less time is available to track them, mistakes increase as everyone is working under pressure and so waste goes up. Before long the spiral becomes vicious. Taking a head in the sand approach when this arises is disastrous.

The first thing to do is to recognise and acknowledge the problem. Take time out to go through it with the team, make sure they fully understand the problem. Listen to their ideas, they will often provide solutions you had not considered. Whatever you do, do not run and hide. This will lead to an enormous fall off in morale amongst the team and quickly spread to your clients or customers.

As the businesses leader it is up to you to set the tone, create the atmosphere that leads to success. I heard a great line from a former Royal Airforce officer many years ago which provides a wonderful flying analogy for how we behave when the going gets tough. "It is your attitude and not your aptitude which determines your altitude."

It always seems ironic these sorts of problems arise because you have been successful. I suspect this is the reason why many choose not to stick their necks out and prefer to operate at a smaller scale and maintain a type of lifestyle business. Real long term success never comes without risk.

Propagating

There frequently comes a time during a business's growth when you will be faced with a decision, a sort of stick or twist occasion if you like. Do you stay with what you have and take a slow steady approach to expansion or do you look to branch out, open up in different locations, export for the first time, add a new product or service, or maybe even sell and move on? Many serial entrepreneurs take this last route, they know what they are good at, they are always more enthused and excited by the new beginning so selling (in whole or part) can release them to the next challenge.

Let's reflect on the journey so far, you have started the business, survived the early trauma's, thrived and grown, throughout your focus will have been very much on working within your business, finding new clients or customers, developing new opportunities and managing those. Now with your initial objectives achieved you are wondering about the future. Perhaps concerned about the amount of time you are spending doing mundane things in the business. Possibly you are even frustrated that you seem unable to do the things you enjoy, very often engaged in tasks that not only you don't like but are not particularly good at. The key to progress is being able to free yourself up to focus on the activities you do well and which brought the enterprise to life in the first place.

For some of course this might be a time to sell up and move on, but assuming you have not reached this point (more on this later) the answer to where you might seek to be in the future lies first with revisiting the original business plan, goals and objectives. In doing so notice how far you have come and now think again about where you would like to be say in three, five or ten years' time. Reset the goals.

At first the new goals might look unrealistic, after all you have an established business, it is demanding too much of your time and energy to run so how on earth can you possibly set bigger goals and set out to achieve them? Well the first thing is to commit to setting them and then commit to the goal, just as you did first time around. What is different now though is you have something that needs to be managed, maintained in order to keep the foundations in place to allow you, the architect and builder, to construct the next phase. Remember "no one is an island." The solution to help you move to the next step is to have the right team around you.

We have talked about getting key people around you to make sure they take on the roles of managing the day to day operations. Sometimes this can be a challenge as the scale of the business might be such that attracting the person you want is difficult. One solution to this of course is applying the same principles of growing to that of selecting your team. If you can bring younger less experienced bright people in early on in the life of your business this will give you the chance to mould and train them to become part of your businesses future and sustainability.

One of the many great attributes of Sir Richard Branson has been his ability to identify and nurture talent, placing them in his businesses to allow them to operate them whilst he moved on to the next exciting challenge. Propagating can mean a number of things, one of the most satisfying can be nurturing talent and allowing it to grow and flourish, in turn this can have an exponential impact on your business.

Another way to propagate is to take part of what you do and multiply it, creating scale.

Multiplication can come in a number of forms as well, from expanding to other sites and locations to franchising or taking part of your business and teaching others in your industry how this can be replicated. It is possible to charge what on the face of it might seem to be considerable sums for this knowledge.

Would anyone pay a "considerable" sum for the knowledge? Doubts are only natural. However is the cost to others really considerable? The headline number you charge might appear big to you, but consider for a moment the time, effort, costly mistakes and the reinvestment and development of what you do, taken in this context suddenly the fee looks reasonable.

If what you pass on saves the buyer time, waste and gets them on the way to their own success quicker the fee will be great value to them.

Value is always what it means to and is seen as in the eye and mind of the buyer, never the seller. You can multiply your business by branching out into other related areas, or add new services or products to your existing range and of course by selling bigger volumes to your existing customers or by selling them additional goods and services. Capital challenges could re- emerge and therefore the question of outside funding becomes something you might need to reconsider if you dismissed it first time around. Branching out can sound exciting (it is believe me..!) and of course be thrilling, but it can also be fraught with danger, especially if this also involves an acquisition.

Over the last 30 years I have come across or witnessed countless situations where organisations have lost considerable sums and wasted a great deal of time seeking to branch out. I often wonder if when the board or company leader thought through their plans if they made the basic mistake I highlighted in the chapter "Pre Match Warm up", which is "do not make the plan or financials fit your idea". It is simply astonishing how often large organisations make this mistake. Ego gets in the way, many CEO's of large corporates get it into their heads that somehow they have the Midas touch, that they are entrepreneurs. Now clearly large corporate boards are running businesses, but often they have never actually built one from the ground up. They have frequently worked their way up a large organisation, become in some respects first class administrators, however successful start-ups tend to be created and kick started by entrepreneurs, not administrators.

That is not to say large corporates do not have entrepreneurs working with in them as of course they do, some large organisations are still lead by their founders. But many are not and some of the mistakes you need to avoid have been made by large corporates.

The first example I recall was an attempt by major insurance groups in the UK to capture larger amounts of market share for the sale and distribution of mortgage linked endowment policies and other life insurance. This was based on the belief that estate agencies were the best place to sell these products to would be homebuyers, after all, where do you go to buy a house?

As I wasn't involved I must speculate as to the answer some boards came up with to this question. Certainly based on the outcomes it is not unreasonable to suspect this was the only question these companies asked themselves. I can almost hear the conversation;

"Surely this must be an easy sale, a young coupe seeking to buy a house have a strong emotional connection to the new property and therefore with the estate agent. Who better to help them arrange the mortgage and the life insurance? Estate agencies up and down the country have tie ups with building societies, insurance brokers and all manner of insurance agencies, so bringing this all together creating efficiencies can only lead to one thing right? More distribution of our products."

At first glance there is a certain logic to this, but this also seems to be the point where common sense and planning went out of the window. As soon as one insurer announced its intention to enter this world another tried to leap on the same bandwagon. As the competition to buy agencies intensified so the multiple of earnings being paid shot up. Simple economics of supply and demand.

Deals went through that allowed the selling agents to pocket large sums and ride off into the sunset. But wait a minute weren't these agents the very people who would have the relationship with the buyer?

I can only assume the insurers thought this of no importance, perhaps they assumed it would be easy to train young hungry estate agents to sell lots of insurance.

Wrong, it's not easy at all.

This was but one error, the event that killed much of this off was the severe downturn in the UK economy and the subsequent collapse in the housing market. House prices right across the UK had become massively over inflated, the fall and then the price recovery actually took close to 10 years. The whole ill conceived enterprise fell apart as house sales and valuations dropped, with mounting job losses so repossessions increased. With their financial losses increasing some of the insurers decided to cut their losses and sold their estate agency chains back to the original owners for a pittance, I recall one being for one Pound.

Another re-purchase for one Pound occurred when a client of mine, for the sake of the tale I will call him Jack, although though this is not his real name bought back his old company for this sum, before we met so I can claim no credit !

Jack had sold out to a larger organisation which itself had plans to take over the world of IT. Jack's business was not the same as the buyers although it operated in a largely compatible sector; they sold a very specific range of software solutions to a very specific market. They understood their market inside and out.

The acquirer thought Jack's business would complement their own perfectly and enable them to create a bigger business; they could also increase profitability with a few efficiency savings. An ambitious move and whilst I am all in favour of ambition, it is important to keep your ego in check. Like the insurers with their estate agency purchases the buyer thought they knew more about running his business than Jack did. They thought changing how it operated and did business would be better. They were wrong, very wrong in fact.

The end came swiftly and Jack together with his colleagues bought their old business back, with its debt for one Pound. It took some toil to turn things back around but eventually they did and some years later found a more sensible larger partner to buy them out. The deal was constructed properly and over time the business was successfully merged into the buyers and although renamed and refined many times since the core product is still out there today being bought and used by corporate customers all over the country.

It is very easy to let ego run away with you, if a successful business is attractive enough to you to buy, surely it is worth considering what made it successful in the first place? Assuming you know better and just making wholesale and radical changes is an enormous risk, too many changes to quickly risks alienating both customers and staff.

Clearly I am not in a position to be definitive about the planning that went into these situations, what I can be sure of is that any step into branching out or an acquisition requires the same thinking process and planning that created your success in the first place, such that it enabled you to even consider expansion through acquisition. If necessary take yourself off somewhere quiet, go back through the steps discussed earlier and then consider the questions from earlier in this chapter:

- What am I seeking to achieve?
- What do I need to know to progress?
- What resources, human, financial or otherwise do I need?
- What does success look like?

I would add these:

- What do I know?
- What should I know?
- What do I want to know?

As I write this I am in the early stages of discussing an acquisition myself. There are some very obvious opportunities for my business, but there are some risks and dangers. Having previously made an acquisition and in truth not being quite so thorough as I am encouraging you to be (or that I am being now) I know all too well what can go wrong.

My personal experience occurred nearly 14 years ago. Just over 12 months after I made the acquisition it is fair to say things were not going well. I succeeded in adding to the demands on my business infrastructure, demands that it could not handle, I had increased debt and not won enough new business from the acquired business. As a result of reflecting on my first year I did two things quite quickly I got in some outside help which for my business at that time was a considerable investment and so I had to find ways to cut the marketing and sales costs without fatally damaging the flow of new business.

Over the following six months with the coach I took on we went back to the beginning and re planned. Not everything I had done was wrong indeed some things were just what the business needed. However there were a number of small faults that meant I was headed off in the wrong direction, just fractionally, but enough that could have resulted in me arriving far from my intended destination.

Looking back and with the benefit of hindsight for me the biggest mistake was not to review the plan soon enough. The first six months had been ridiculously busy and costly. At the time the lack of revenue growth did not worry me, I put it down to the teething problems we were having. But had I reviewed things more carefully (and been a little more attentive to the KPI's) rather than making assumptions I would have spotted some early signs. Interestingly this period also coincided with a time when I had not been using a coach or mentor. This is not a mistake I have made since.

- Remember hindsight does not pay the bills.

The bright side of this experience of course is not only did we turn things around but grew the business to the point that I actually sold part of the business in 2011 as part of a strategy to allow us to move in a slightly different direction and grow the business further.

It would be remiss of me to end this chapter without some reference to ways of building new business opportunities. This can be interesting at all kinds of levels, not least because there is no single way that necessarily makes more sense than any other.

As with my remarks in the chapter "Pre Match Warm up", it is tempting in this day and age to assume that technology provides all of the answers. It doesn't or least not all of the time. Being blindsided by technology causes many to ignore or with the very young not even realise there are some basic fundamentals that hold true regardless of technology. They were true when the first locomotives became the disruptive technology of their time. The locomotive or steam train by changing the way goods and people could be moved changed not only the way things could be done, i.e. more, further, faster, but opened up new opportunities. One trade that expanded enormously in the UK was the cotton and clothing trade. However it did not mean that selling clothing needed a locomotive. The new method of transport might have made distribution to wider markets possible but it did not change what was needed to manufacture and sell clothes.

Today I watch younger members of my team when seeking a solution to something dive into, in fact almost scramble for their smart phone. If you don't believe me try asking several younger members of your own team or friends a question that you do not have the answer to (or one you do know the answer to can provide another interesting test as to accuracy of course) I guarantee they will race each other to find it online.

I am always fascinated by the speed they can get a search sorted. One of them will give you the answer another might have a variation or different answer. However it plays out they will almost all come up with roughly the same answer within seconds of each other. Sadly this is precisely how they seek to do everything.

The temptation for the young is that the answer to everything in life lies online. They will assume when starting a new enterprise or breaking out in a new direction within an existing business or enterprise that the answer can be found on the internet; chances are it won't, or if they find the answer it is likely it will be fairly poor quality advice in a chat room or blog. The very best advice online is like any other commodity it needs to be paid for, so beware the free answers.

One very interesting anecdote I came across recently involves the England Rugby Union team which recruited a specialist coach to work with the players to improve their visual awareness. The coach Dr. Sherylle Calder, blames the smartphone for the decline in awareness and hand eye coordination. I took this quote form the UK newspaper the Daily Telegraph "We are losing the ability to communicate well and all those skills are declining. We will be working really hard on awareness because awareness helps you make effective decisions under pressure."

Getting your product or service out there will need you to focus on the same things that have worked for decades.

Essentially any product or service that addresses a particular need, solves a problem or creates a new opportunity should be saleable, yet some businesses actually struggle because they cannot obtain or close enough sales. Or they can't produce enough sales at the right margin.

No matter whether your business is a new online solution, website, app or a more traditional product or service you will first need to make the world aware of it. There are all sorts of ways of doing this;

- Advertising
- Cold calling
- Exhibitions / events / seminars / trade shows
- Knocking on doors

- Mail shots/ email
- Press / PR
- Networking / social media
- Referral / introduction / word of mouth

Determining the method that best suits you and your business is key of course and some of these will never work for you and some will always work. Others will have times when they are very helpful and sometimes they will not be. A combination of methods is usually a good idea. You must also be prepared for a little trial and error.

Deploying the right technology can make each of these work more effectively, it can also lead you up the garden path if you are not careful. Aside from the third and the last two on the list everything else is a variation on the same theme, that is to say bringing your name or product into the public domain. It can also be a bit hit and miss as to whether or not the information lands with the right people at the right time, which of course is why it needs to be repeated time and time again. Getting this type of marketing right can be difficult and it usually pays to get some help. Beware web companies telling you how marvellous they are at search engine optimisation, this is ultimately no more effective than making sure your advertisement is in the right part of a publication. It is of no use whatsoever if your product or service is something new that no one realises they need yet.

It is quite interesting that insurance aggregators, holiday company's and hotel websites spend fortunes on old fashioned media to drive business to their website!

Advertising can be expensive and a very easy way to waste or lose money. However as can be seen by the proliferation of advertising it must work enough of the time to have businesses invest in it. Henry Ford famously declared that fifty percent of his advertising worked, he just did not know which fifty percent. Just as it was true for Ford in the past so it is today.

Seeking good advice ahead of any major advertising spend is probably wise, but what if you are starting up and do not have the budget?

The answer is to come back to some very basic questions (yes those again..), what are you trying to achieve? What do you know? What do you need to know or find out? Planning is just as important with this as it is with anything.

Advertising often breaks into two broad categories, name awareness or a call to action. The travel companies I mentioned are doing no more than seeking to make you are well aware of their name, so that next time you use a search engine to locate a hotel online and their name comes up you will recognise it, it will feel familiar. Other adverts frequently found on cable or satellite channels have a very direct call to action, for example. *"If you buy this specially created CD (yes some folk still listen to CD's) music collection by the end of the week we will throw in an extra CD for free."* Or it might be the latest foody trend brought to you by a clever new piece of kitchen equipment. This latter advertising will also go to great lengths to tell you about the product features or some unique point it has.

Clearly there are other advertisers that are seeking both to generate name awareness and a call to action, car manufacturers being one obvious example. Where they ensure their name is repeated over and over whilst also highlighting something amazing about the product or price that sets it apart, with a time limited offer. Furniture suppliers are probably the most prominent uses of this method in the UK.

All this is great, but as I asked earlier how can this help a small start up? Frankly, it can't. So assuming you have answered the questions I raised and you understand the answers fully, then it is possible to get something more targeted and lower cost organised.

I have not advertised for years, yet early in my career I ran a twice weekly advert that proved to be quite successful. Firstly I had to advertise. I had no customers to get introductions or testimonials from, no exhibitions for months that I could attend and few networking opportunities. I did some cold calling and door knocking as well but I needed to have another strand so turned to advertising.

I had a service that addressed a very high demand market that also happened to be a market with few available solutions. To begin with I put the advert together myself (although I did copy a couple of others I liked) and I ran it in a local newspaper. The advert had my picture in it and offered a free consultation, plus my telephone number. That was it; and it worked, or at least lots of people called and came in for a free consultation!

Then what happened?

Well most of those that came to see me had already been everywhere else first and could not get what they wanted. Some of course had not so I was able to do some business with these people quite quickly. We did a good enough job that word spread, in time more of those who came in had not been everywhere else first, we became the first port of call.

For those who did use us as a last resort I was able to do one of two things or sometimes both. Firstly if I could find an innovative or new solution I would. Secondly whether I did or not I was able to cement a good enough relationship that I began, albeit very slowly, to acquire names and addresses of people who would need me at some time or another. Those names made it into a mail list and they also received our quarterly newsletter. Today of course you would most likely stay in touch via email, although do not discount the occasional written contact, particularly if your customer is slightly older or is a business that only ever receives electronic contact. The novelty of the post cannot be under estimated.

In time of course the advertising became less effective. Also it was hard work in the beginning as I was meeting lots of people for free that I could not help. But you can only reap what you sow; with a growing number of new customers so it became easier to use other means of generating leads.

We also did exhibitions and tradeshows, which of course can be very hard work, but also very enjoyable. If you have ever done them or been to one I am sure you will have seen or experienced the initial enthusiasm which after the first long day or two begins to wane as tiredness creeps in, the repetition of your message becomes tedious and your enthusiasm flags.

Doing this for yourself though can be a great motivator to persist and see it through, as the show gets towards its end and fewer people are wandering around so your competitors (especially those working for someone else) start to leave the stand empty for long periods of time. That can be a godsend for you, so hang in there.

The very first one I did was in the late 1980's in the role I had before starting on my own business. I was on a small stand at the end of a centre row. Opposite occupying the whole of the corner and part of the side was a much larger and far swankier stand. They were selling DIY equipment, the exhibitor was for a very long established well known UK chain; on two nights (it was a long show, four days, 10am – 10pm) they had the then recently retired world light heavyweight boxing champion John Conteh on their stand (what a great guy, but that is a different story), not only was he a well known face in Britain but a natural at speaking to the crowd, a cross between a market trader and skilled raconteur. He was so good the crowed filled the space between the stand and at times no one could get past. What's more no one was too interested in the other stands. He was taking their trade, or at least that is what some said and moaned about. Since most of the people gathered could see next to nothing of what he was doing I would engage them in conversation about what he was doing. I would even invite them onto my stand to get a better view. We would reminisce about Conteh the boxer or discuss the perils of DIY, I never tried to sell them anything; I would have been wasting my time. However no one I spoke to left without a card or entering the champagne draw we were holding. John Conteh was the best draw my stand had. Oh, if you are not a boxing fan or are not old enough, look him up online, great bloke, great boxer.

There were two choices that week, curse my misfortune at having him across the aisle as many did, or find a way to maximise the chance, innovate. Thinking on your feet is sometimes essential to business success.

By the time I started out in my own business I had sufficient contacts and clients to get things moving quite quickly. As we built up a greater number of clients so we began to hold small quarterly events, these were intended to be an opportunity to communicate with existing clients and for them to invite friends or colleagues as their guest. Whilst this objective was achieved something else happened I had not considered in advance, the attendees were also networking with each other. Not only did this generate me new business but lots of kudos as people often remember just how and when they met particularly if this gives rise to a flourishing business relationship. These are things I do to this day.

However as they have become increasingly popular and people I seek to invite are being asked to go to more and more things, so now I do this quite sparingly and we also make sure we do something just a little different, whether that is the venue, or some form of entertainment.

The main point is to try to come up with something that people might not do on their own accord.

Mass market seminars have been a great way to create new leads in a variety of service industries over the years. However as with anything that works well so the market becomes crowded and invitations to seminars land in peoples letter boxes or email inbox all the time. If you take this route prepare to take longer to get the volume of new business you have heard others achieve in the past. Patently it still works, but fewer people attend than in the past and the lead in time to closing business is often quite long. That said if you continue to do them over time you will build a steady pipeline of opportunity and so it becomes a game of persistence and patience.

The alternative is to be more targeted. One of the reasons for the events I arranged early in my first business was down to not having access to sufficient data to mass mail invitations. The data I could get was absurdly expensive and of course the cost of printing and mailing were very high in those days. Today each stage is much cheaper. So what we actually put on is typically a cross between a seminar and an event.

It could be worth thinking about a hybrid for your business. If you are in a service industry then a breakfast briefing of no more than an hour if you are targeting business clients or customers. If what you do is direct to consumer consider lunchtime or evening. Make sure you provide something useful, some information or advice that they receive without cost. Not the whole solution obviously but enough to be helpful and also enough to give them incentive to return for the rest.

A manufacturer could do the same for a product launch, rather than an expensive trade stand why not put on an event at your own place of business? Provide good quality outside catering and perhaps a short talk of interest to your customers on an unrelated topic. The chances are this will both be less costly than an expensive day at the races and much more effective. Be different, innovate, vary what you do. However be careful not to be so good at the event or the advertising that the only thing anyone remembers is the event or the advert. There was one classic in the UK that ran in the late 1970's and early 1980's starring Joan Collins and the late Leonard Rossiter, it was so good few people could remember the product often confusing it with another well known aperitif. For the record the advert was for Cinzano.

Networking is a good way of getting yourself known in the business community. However be careful, pushing your product the instant you meet someone new as it can be the ultimate turn off. Also beware with regular networking events or groups set up for the specific purpose of networking. My experience has been that in time you will only see the same faces time and again. These things seem to have a finite life.

One event I attended regularly in London a few years ago was run by a group of Venture Capitalists, they combined a number of the things I alluded to earlier, refreshment, an interesting speaker and an opportunity to mingle and introduce yourself to someone new. I was in the habit of taking a client with me, dangerous you might think as there were competitors in the room, however this was not the case, firstly I chose the clients I invited carefully. I wanted to take people who had something to gain by going; for them what they saw was an opportunity they would not otherwise have had. Since there was nothing directly in it for me it served to cement their loyalty not threaten our work together. One client actually met an engineer seeking help with a business, my client was not only able to provide that help, but furthermore invest in the company. His return on that investment has been twenty times, do you suppose he has forgotten how he came to have that opportunity? Over the six or seven years since then he has become one of the best advocates I could ever have wished for. The risk was tiny and the cost non existent.

Networking is not a natural place for everyone, in a recent issue of his regular column in the Daily Telegraph newspaper founder and Chairman of Timpson's, John Timpson says as much, but he also provides some sage advice for networkers. "A bit of networking is good for you, but don't make it a full time job."

Using the press and getting good coverage can be invaluable, for most of the time its impact is quick and short lived, there are some cases where this is not the case, Gerald Ratner comes to mind, but generally it is the case that the results do not live long in the mind. Once again cost can be an issue especially for an early stage business. However local publications are usually screaming out for content. So an approach to your local newspaper or magazine, all of which also have online content these days can bear fruit. If you can write your own piece so much the better sometimes they will run them unedited.

An alternative if you are advertising is to send in a press release making an announcement or ask the paper if they would like to interview you. I have done all these, independently and in combination and found that mostly they work. An ongoing PR campaign can be costly, but in the early stages of your business you can achieve a surprising amount yourself. If writing is not your thing, then look around your team, family and friends to see if anyone can help. One thing will become apparent, the process gets easier the more you do. Practice is crucial at any aspect of running and building your business. The South African golfer Gary Player when he was at the height of his career said, "The more I practice the luckier I get."

Obtaining introductions and referrals is without doubt the most cost effective way of gaining new business. However it seems to be something that people struggle with or in some cases simply cannot obtain at all. I have heard and read more clever, razzle dazzle sales techniques to obtain referrals than I could write down; as with many things in life most manage to over complicate a very simple, although not necessarily easy thing. Fundamentally you need two things, first you need to be "referable" and second you need to ask.

Being referable is pretty easy really, for me this is as much about how you conduct yourself and of course how you conduct business. I would recommend you make sure you do three things (do it anyway, it just makes sense.);

- Be punctual. Not just getting to meetings on time, but in delivery. Do not make promises for timescales that you cannot guarantee meeting. It is tempting if you need the revenue, but just don't do it. If someone else or another business or businesses are likely to impact on your delivery timescales, factor this in, then add some time. Position it with your customer or client, make sure they understand.
- Be polite. Being polite and courteous costs nothing and helps convey respect. These are reflective behaviours, the more you do it the deeper the level of respect that is returned.

- Complete what you start. Again this is so basic and yet seems to be difficult for people to do. How often have you been promised something in business and it not happen? Avoid this at all costs.

Having made sure you conduct yourself in the right manner it will give you the capacity I would almost say the authority to ask. If you do a good job for someone why wouldn't they spread the word?

So how do you ask?

In this chapter we have already looked at some subtle ways of asking, client events are a great way of getting existing customers or clients to introduce you to people. Very often the biggest challenge to overcome with referrals is the client themselves not knowing how to do it, this approach eliminates that completely.

Being very specific and targeted in asking also helps the client to think about who they can approach. For example if you have a product or service that has a very specific market or demographic, discussing those specifics with your client whilst encouraging them to think about the other people he or she might know with a similar problem can lead you to asking them to introduce you. If your request is too general about your work then they are most likely to say they cannot think of anyone. Of course they can't as you did not provide a sufficiently focussed situation or narrow enough reason.

Another route is to seek out a source of prospective introductions who has both access to your target market and with whom you can build trust in your solution or product. This can sometimes be a slow burn and will require considerable effort. In my own career I have sought out professional advisors in different sectors. I have not only sought to establish a good working relationship and mutual trust but I have gone out of my way to try to find them work, there is nothing more potent in these types of situation than being a provider of opportunity, it very much keeps you in the forefront of their thinking. Make sure you stay in regular contact, updating them on new product lines or specific issues that you come across that might be of use or interest to them.

Harvest and Reward

I t is in the nature of writing that we must set things in an order, so in some senses this chapter could be argued to be out of order. I would hope on your business journey you have been able to reap some reward before now.

At the risk of contradicting myself, there is considerable merit of thinking about the long term plans for your enterprise early in its life. Is this something that you will seek to exit at some future date with a sale or even an IPO? Or do you have ambitions for your business to become a family enterprise, or like mine to have people join your business who become equity participants and over time foster your own buyout.

It does not really matter which, but thinking this through relatively early can enhance the chances of getting it right. Part of my business has been dedicated to helping business owners plan their exit and I have dealt with all three situations. I will come onto some examples shortly but first I would like to set out the case for planning the rules of your company, not the business it is in and how it does what it does and for whom as we are long past that by now, I hope. Rather I mean the company's own rules, any registered limited company will have its Memorandum and Articles of Association few though have shareholder agreements.

At first glance you might logically assume that the Memorandum will deal with this, but most company formations use a standard set of paragraphs and are limited to dealing with matters such as what constitutes a quorum for a directors meeting or how directors are to be remunerated.

Other matters such as conflicts of interest and how shareholder meetings, AGM's or EGM's are to be constituted.

These standard documents do not go far enough. It is very important to think through your objectives, use the questions in previous chapters to help. Once you have written these down, they might appear almost like a letter of wishes for a Will, indeed the type of agreement I have in mind is often referred to as a company Will. This document would include things such as what happens when a shareholder / director dies or becomes ill. How minor shareholders are to be treated, sometimes called "drag along" provisions. The agreement would also restrict how and when shares could be sold and to whom. Unlike the Memorandum and Articles of Association however these are not legal requirements.

Knowing how you plan to exit a business before you have it up and running might seem a little silly and certainly I do not think you should be rushing to do this. Conversely leaving it to the last minute is absurd and poses significant financial risk to the founder.

For reasons of confidentiality I have amended the names, business sector and scale of the examples I am about to provide. My aim here is to illustrate the things that can and do go awry.

My first example concerns a client who had acquired his business via a management buyout about ten years prior to seeking to exit for retirement. Let's call him Dave, again not his real name.

The business was highly specialised, long established and had a good reputation. There were two sides to the company, a manufacturing side and a repair / refurbishment element. The latter being a vital cashflow diversifier when the economic cycle impacted the manufacturing side. The business was not huge, almost a lifestyle business with a small staff of around twenty employees. The owner really needed to be an integral part of the operations as things stood. The capacity to grow the business was limited in that it operated in a very small market of which it had a sizeable share.

I had only been dealing with Dave's affairs for a very limited time, ironically following my own purchase of another business of which he was a client. He had a very specific issue that required our attention which resulted in limited amounts of time being spent on the future planning and his objectives. He rebutted any discussion about his business and exit plans until we could get the matter troubling him most resolved. It took some time to do this and once we had I asked Dave about his plans for the company.

He was somewhat surprised that I should be asking, firstly he was not close to retirement age, nor in fact did he want to stop what he was doing. He had only just repaid the money he had borrowed to buy the business and despite his having grown the revenue he had not benefitted hugely from the upturn in finances. Something he wanted to do, which clearly he was both entitled to and able too, so I encouraged him.

Never the less I did discuss with him the need to think about his exit, as his children were not interested in joining the business. Selling such a specialist company was unlikely to be easy and certainly not quick unless anyone on the team would seek to buy. A member of the existing team buying was improbable as Dave himself had been the only person when employed by the previous owner with the desire to do a deal and buy in the first place. Furthermore he had effectively made his old role redundant and merged it with that of the original owner when he bought the business. This provided both an immediate improvement to the bottom line and of course the means to settle the debt, but no obvious candidate to affect a management buyout.

Dave did at least agree to a meeting with a boutique corporate finance business that specialises in selling small businesses. Although the meeting went well, nothing came of the proffered service to assist with shaping the business such that it would be attractive to a potential buyer.

Given his age and that of his wife I anticipated the period between these discussions and him actually exiting would be several years, so I was utterly stunned not only when Dave announced that he was aiming to sell but had found a buyer! Worse still he had agreed the price and essentially concluded the means by which the transaction would take place, based on a valuation he himself and the buyer determined, all without referring back to the corporate finance house I mentioned or seeking any independent advice on any aspect of the transaction.

The bad news kept coming, Dave had agreed to remain with the business for several months to affect a handover on his normal salary and he agreed to act as banker. Yes that's right he was going to provide the finance for the buyer to acquire his business.

In simple terms the deal was to be constructed as a management buy in. He was going to be paid on a deferred basis over three years. In some respects not unlike the deal he made when buying himself. However there were a few serious differences, firstly when Dave carried out his own buyout he had worked for the firm for a couple of years, he knew and understood the business very well. His previous working life had provided him with the necessary skills not only to work on the business, but in the business should it be needed.

The buyer in this case was someone my client barely knew, he had no experience in manufacturing and could only partially replace my client in the areas of general management, so an additional person would need to be hired to take on much of Dave's role. In theory taking the management head count back to where it had been when Dave had bought the business. Whilst Dave's original buyout had been fashioned over several years, the new deal was to take place over a much shorter timescale putting extra pressure on the company cashflow.

Worse was to follow; soon after the deal was signed the business ran into difficulty, not through any mismanagement, but the economic downturn caused by the credit crisis. Dave ended up doing two things, returning to work to keep the business going and taking a deferral on the already deferred payments. Fortunately the buyer was both honourable and hard working. The revised deal included interest payments and in time the full consideration was met. The company has survived and indeed continued to grow. Dave eventually got his capital, but for a time it was touch and go. Professional advice might not be cheap, but imagine the consequences if this had not worked out.

This whole chain of events occurred almost as if the meeting with the corporate finance people had never taken place. It all reminded me of another business transaction that a client took part in as the buyer some twenty years earlier. This one did not end well; sadly for the employees of the business and the client the business failed during a previous economic downturn. The seller had deferred some consideration and he too lost that.

This particular example involved virtually no planning at all, no thought as to the capability of the buyer at running the business. As with the previous case my client had worked at the firm for some time. Although he had an intimate knowledge of the company's activity, he was not a business manager. These were facts that could have been established by all concerned at outset; careful thought could have led to a more satisfactory outcome.

If the deal had been put together with the involvement of someone capable of managing the business in addition to the buyers undoubted skills at making the workshop function and provide excellent results for customers the outcome would have been so very different.

As the seller of a business therefore it is just as important to consider the qualities of your would be buyer as it is incumbent on the buyer to understand the business, its finances and future opportunities. Due diligence is not just something that the buyer undertakes to make sure they are paying the right price and of course are acquiring an opportunity and not a liability. The seller, particularly if there is some element of deferred consideration (which there often is these days) must make sure the buyer has the skills to deliver, if not then it may be necessary to consider a lower sale price to receive full settlement at outset. Or do not sell, but look for a buyer who can both meet the financial obligations and also ensure that the business continues. In my view there is a moral obligation of course to your people, the team that helped you build the business in the first place. Is it right to take the money and run whilst exposing the people left behind to the perils of an inexperienced or worse even an incompetent buyer?

It is clearly impossible to cover every risk, but it is quite possible to mitigate most and eliminate many with thought and planning. What is also needed when thinking about selling is time; time to make sure all of the necessary steps can and do take place, time to organise the business so it is attractive to a potential buyer i.e. It is solidly based, has good repeatable cashflow and future growth prospects. Trying to sell a company with no upside for the buyer can only lead to a depressed valuation at sale.

Typically most SME businesses (the definition of small or medium sized enterprises means something completely different to lots of people, for my purposes I have assumed small to be a business valued at less than £1 million and medium being those over this level) owners will first seek guidance as to value from their accountant. Fair enough you might think, but sadly this can be a mistake. The more far sighted accountants will tend to seek specialist help, frequently from outside their own firm when valuing a company. Larger firms of accountants may well have a corporate finance arm in house. Whatever situation you find yourself in it is important to seek the help of an expert at valuing and selling businesses.

Choosing advisors and a corporate finance house can be a little bit like restaurants there is a huge variance in quality and not always can you rely on cost being the clue to quality. Some of the worst in this field are among the more expensive. The ones to beware of tend to be specialist business selling agencies, they will unquestionably promise that they can deliver the highest valuation for you, usually quicker than anyone else and frequently they will claim to have access to a vast resource of potential buyers for your type of business all over the globe. If in addition to this there is a huge upfront fee and retainer then tread more carefully still. That is not to say these firms cannot deliver, clearly they do, but one of the reasons for the large fees is their success rate tends to be quite low. They often have a vast marketing machine to feed and so need to guarantee the fee income, hence the upfront and retainer costs. Choosing an advisor with some form of contingent fee built into the success of the sale is likely to mean you have someone focussed on your outcome, with your mutual interests being aligned.

Regardless of how you choose to sell the process can be painful and frequently takes much longer than anyone realises. For the small business the distraction can be huge. Several years ago I sold part of my own business, the objective was simple, I had been struggling to manage an increasingly unwieldy firm and the solution to growing was in my view to shrink the enterprise first. Whilst the strategy has ultimately proved correct, more than once I thought I was making a huge mistake.

The primary challenge was going through the sales process, due diligence and other aspects of the sale process at the same time as keeping new business moving forwards. Sadly the latter suffered. Recovery took much long than I anticipated, not least because during the many months of the process I was paying insufficient attention to new opportunities, with just the time available to manage existing business and the sale process.

The reason for raising this is to make a vital point to would be sellers. If you become distracted whilst preparing and going through the sale process you can find yourself with an unwanted problem.

I can best illustrate this by drawing on an example a client experienced only last year. Together with a colleague he was close to completing a management buy in and management buyout or to use the vernacular BIMBO. The process had been going along fairly swimmingly or at least as swimmingly as these things ever get. The valuation was agreed the mechanism for payment and the element of value that was to be paid by deferred consideration set. Accountants and lawyers had been appointed to deal with the due diligence. This was not the type of deal to make the front pages of the newspapers, but nor was it tiny. The company was valued at several million pounds and so with it came a degree more complexity than might be the case for a smaller enterprise. The buyers, needed and wanted to know everything they could possibly know, down to how much the company was spending on paperclips. Part of the valuation included an element based on the future revenue and the work the firm had in progress. In some service based sectors this might be considered goodwill. To coin a phrase this is where the fight started.

Very close to the end of the process it became apparent to the buyers that the forecast revenue was going to fall well short of predictions, furthermore the owners had ceased (or been distracted as I was with my sale) to seek out and exploit new business opportunities. The result being that the valuation placed on the business now looked inflated. Not unreasonably the buyers wanted to return to the negotiating table. Somewhat less reasonably the seller did not and was holding out for the agreed price, even though much of the valuation had been based on a promised revenue stream that wasn't there, the would be buyers walked away and the deal fell over.

So whilst we may all be very familiar with the term caveat emptor or buyer beware, this term can equally be applied to the seller who must be equally attentive and aware.

Get your exit planning right and everyone will be happy, get it wrong and someone and potentially everyone will lose out. If in doubt think about the conversation you will have with your loved ones after you have failed to sell.

This is by no means the only example, indeed I have too many to write about! One other I will go over best highlights what can happen when you leave to little future opportunity for a buyer. I visited a business several years ago, it was a small family run business that was with the second generation. There was no third generation so succession was off the table. The business provided a variety of exhibition and signage products, it had a loyal solid customer base, a similarly solid workforce and the market was unlikely to find itself badly disrupted by new technology, but similarly it was quite mature, operated in a very competitive environment so massive future growth was unlikely. The business as was somewhere between a lifestyle business and an enterprise capable of expanding if for example a trade buyer or forward thinking member of the current team chose to diversify and leverage the customer relationships.

Sometime before I met them the subject of a sale had been raised by the owners with the team and one member of the workforce had indicated a willingness to buy. Given the solid nature of the business and his experience within it, the risk to the buyer was not enormous. I am unsure whether he had the desire to grow things or not, but a combination of his age and skill suggested to me that he would do just fine. For some reason however the owners decided now was not the time to sell, they kept deferring a decision.

Part of their problem I believe was not being able to truly decide what they wanted. When I went to see them it was concerning a very specific need, they had their minds very much on a future project which needed funding, unfortunately they did not have sufficient funds of their own, added to which, business had slowed and to make matters worse (and perhaps not surprisingly) the proposed MBO was faltering, due to the mixed messages coming from the owners. I provided them with some outline thoughts and ideas. Clearly they were not appealing enough as they did nothing.

We stayed in touch over the year that followed, but the last time I spoke to them the business had not sold and had to all intents and purposes become a lifestyle business which was being slowly run down. A combination of not planning, waiting too long to sell and basically being greedy (in terms of taking maximum out of the business over the years) left them with nowhere to go. The business had quite quickly become worth much less than they would like, it was arguably worthless.

It can be costly, painful and infuriating when a buyer walks away from a deal, the buyer has the option. A seller can become too dependent on the sale and can blow it quickly.

I am not trying to suggest the process of a sale and planning for it is easy, far from it, but just because something is difficult or challenging does not mean ignoring it will solve the problem. Any business that has survived long enough to be saleable must have at some time come through challenging times and by definition so have the directors and owners. The plain truth is whatever the issues they can be tackled, it just takes the courage to get on with it.

PROMOTION AND SUCCESSION

This chapter is actually very much part of the previous one, however I wanted to devote something specifically towards family enterprises. Many SME's up and down the UK are family run enterprises, from small tradesman and artisan businesses to much large organisations. Some are incredibly old, several years ago I had the privilege to provide advice to a family company that was in its 175th year of operation. The youngest members of the board being capable of keeping it going for at least another 40 or 50 years, I hope they do.

There is so much that can and probably needs to be said about family business and succession that in the short space here I may not do the subject full justice. There are however some very simple (not necessarily easy..!) steps to take when considering family succession. At the risk of becoming repetitive you can probably guess the first. You need to plan.

Consideration and thought about what succession might look like needs to take place far sooner than you might realise.

Often I have known situations where parents have been profoundly disappointed that their children have shown little or no interest in the family business. Usually it has been too late in the lives of all concerned for me to make real enquiries and suggest a course that might result in a change. Conversely I have come across situations where family conflict has resulted from younger family members joining the business.

Often what these situations tend to have in common is a lack of engagement by the younger members of the family, with careful thought and planning this can be overcome. It is important early on to seek engagement of younger members of the family. Sometimes they simply won't want to follow mum and dad into the business. It is important not to take this as some sort of slight on the older generation, but assuming they will follow in your footsteps is a mistake, you need to talk to them about it and do it early. Finding out when you have time to consider a different course of action is imperative to a successful outcome.

Assuming the family want to be involved and depending on their ages, it is important to introduce them to the family firm, what it does and how. Let them see the inspiring parts and develop their own interest. It is surely better to find out early and be happy with the outcome, that the children are not interested? Do not assume because they show interest as youngsters that their school subject choices and university education will not cause them to make other decisions.

Choice is a crucial part of this, trying to force your kid's into the business is not remotely intelligent.

About six years ago I had a meeting with the Finance Director of a long established family business in the Midlands. He and the Chief Operating Officer had responsibility for the day to day running of the firm, however the ultimate executive power lay with the Chairman. He was an elderly man, he had three children and apparently (I have never met him so I have to take the FD's word for this) was determined they would inherit and run the business. There was just one small problem, the children had no interest and had each developed their own lives.

Sadly the Chairman and majority shareholder seemed utterly oblivious to this fact, he had inherited from his father and his equally elderly sister had a small shareholding. It was almost as if he believed that the children would simply be forced to run the business when they inherit the stock following his inevitable death. Whilst something might change it seems highly probable that when he does die the business will be sold. I might be wrong of course, but assuming I am not the current full time managers at the time of my meeting were not interested in a buyout and were in effect minding the shop and making sure they stayed in work. The odds that this company will remain independent or sell for anything like its true worth are remote.

However much it might be human nature that we frequently choose to avoid the question because we fear the answer, burying our head in the sand is not a smart thing to do. Yes these conversations can take courage, not just in posing the questions, but in accepting an answer you may not want to hear.

In a sense having these conversations with younger family members early in their lives is just a normal part of their growing up. Parents taking an interest in their dreams and aspirations, if those are towards the business then seeking out the right school and university courses to meet that objective is likely to be helpful. There is also considerable merit in them not joining the business immediately (this may depend on the size of the firm) but to go and work elsewhere first, getting a broad understanding of business outside the family silo. Conversely pushy parenting is likely to drive children in the opposite direction to the one we are keen on promoting.

Dealing with all of the issues of succession or exit early is crucial. Unplanned an exit from your business in whatever form it takes, can be very costly as it is all too easy to make mistakes. Whatever you do please don't do it without advice, an independent valuation and legal advice on the documentation before you sign anything. Yes this does happen a client once confessed to me he signed a legally binding heads of terms without advice, fortunately although there was something in the agreement that could have been costly in a different transaction this time it proved not so painful. But a valuable lesson that served him well in the future.

CONCLUSION

Although there are notable exceptions most business books are too long. By definition entrepreneurs are busy people of mind and body so a weighty volume is most likely to go unread regardless of its quality. Clearly it is my hope that this book has uses for you. Before closing I want to refresh you on one or two things and also add four essential things you must do with your business in order to succeed. None of these are silver bullets, that is to say they cannot guarantee your success. However not doing them will increase the risk of failure.

All successful business start with an idea, however an idea on its own is like a car without fuel, useless and going nowhere. The fuel you need is to understand what you want to achieve. The first steps to take are to plan, ask yourself the questions in the chapter

"Pre Match Warm up." Develop a plan, spend time visualising your success. Look at the resources you will need to get the business up and running and enable it to be sustained. Above all else make sure;

- Your revenue is greater than costs. Model the cashflow, look at your pricing, is it right? If you cannot sell what you produce for more than it costs to make, ditch it and go back to the beginning. Remember do not fall in love with your idea to your financial detriment.
- Look after the cashflow. Get the invoices out on time and the revenue collected. A business with a strong order book and no money is not likely to survive for long.
- Put your customer outcome at the centre of the business. Make sure you delight and look after the customer and they in turn will look after you.
- Your people are your most valuable business asset, look after them and ensure they are engaged in the enterprise.

If you have found this helpful, or you would like to download a free business planner then please do visit our website www.rossmiddleton.co.uk where you will find various articles and links that may be helpful to you. For more reading the following are worth the investment and time:

How the best get better - Dan Sullivan and Catherine Nomura

What they don't teach you at Harvard Business School - Mark McCormack

The Best Damn Sales Book Ever – Warren Greshes

The One Minute Entrepreneur - Ken Blanchard, Don Hutson and Ethan Willis

The Four C's. - Dan Sullivan

The Hockey Stick Principles - Bobby Martin

www.ingramcontent.com/pod-product-compliance
Lightning Source LLC
Chambersburg PA
CBHW021441170526
45164CB00001B/338